THE RESTORATION

OF ISRAEL

By

J. Llewellyn Thomas, F.R.C.S

THE COVENANT PUBLISHING COMPANY LIMITED
121 Low Etherley, Bishop Auckland, Co. Durham, DL14 0HA

First edition 1922
Second edition, revised 1930
Third edition, reset and reprinted 2016

ISBN 978-085205-116-0

Printed by
THE COVENANT PUBLISHING COMPANY LIMITED
121, Low Etherley, Bishop Auckland,
Co. Durham, DL14 0HA
www.covpub.co.uk

CONTENTS

FOREWORD

This book is a very methodical study aimed at establishing precisely the meaning of 'The Restoration of Israel' as used in the title. The author defines the terms which are needed to understand the biblical record correctly and takes the reader step by step through the history of the nation and the prophecies pertaining to it.

As the chapter headings indicate, the 'Time,' 'Place,' 'Religion' and 'Population' of Israel are examined carefully in the light of Scripture and the conclusion that the nations of Great Britain and the United States of America are the modern day Ephraim and Manasseh is reached in a compelling way.

The Second Edition of this work was published in 1930 at a time when having emerged from the horrors of the Great War and all the deprivations of the Depression people could begin to look forward to more settled and peaceful times with the British Empire 'an empire that was to stand for ever.'

With the perfect view of hindsight the reader can see that no thought of the future turmoil of the Second World War, the establishment of the Jewish State of Israel and the falling away from the faith had crossed the writer's mind. The time when the "adversary the devil, as a roaring lion, walketh about, seeking whom he may devour" (I *Peter* 5:8) can be seen clearly now and is not yet over. This onslaught of evil threatens to overwhelm Christian civilization itself but great comfort comes from the Promises of God to His people as set out in this book.

Whatever may indeed take place in the future we can rest assured in the words of Almighty God,

"For I am the LORD, I change not; therefore ye sons of Jacob are not consumed" (*Malachi* 3:6).

The Publishers
March, 2016

CHAPTER I

THE RESTORATION OF ISRAEL

CONTENTS

CHAPTER I

THE RESTORATION OF ISRAEL

In considering this subject it is important to know in advance what we exactly mean by the terms "Restoration" and "Israel." It is possible to assign to them, quite correctly, more than one meaning. The word "Restoration" is open, as we shall see, to two meanings, and the same remark applies with even greater force to the term "Israel." Whom do we mean by "Israel"? Let us at once state that the name is used here in its usual, particular and limited sense of Israel of the Ten Tribes, the Ten Tribed northern kingdom of Israel, and does not include the Jewish kingdom of Judah in the south of Palestine.

The two kingdoms of Israel and Judah began their independent existence in 975 BC, after the death of Solomon, and they continued to exist side by side, generally in deadly antagonism, for two and a half centuries, at the close of which time the kingdom of Israel was destroyed while the southern, the Jewish kingdom, continued as a realm for nearly another century and a half. This is an important fact. The Jewish kingdom existed more than half as long again as the kingdom of Israel.

The kingdom of Israel lasted 254 years.
The kingdom of Judah lasted 387 years.
The kingdom of Judah was destroyed by Nebuchadnezzar—
153 years after Pul and Tiglath-Pileser's invasion of Israel.
133 years after Shalmanezer and Sargon's invasion of Israel.

Both kingdoms declined from the worship of Jehovah. The declension of Israel was immediate and rapid, and without any respite; whereas Judah, after many revivals of the true faith, finally declined and fell away after the reign of the good king Josiah.

TABLE NO. I

DURATIONS OF THE KINGDOMS OF ISRAEL AND JUDAH

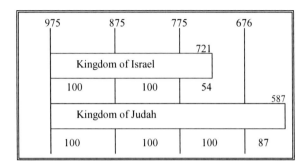

Israel's decline began when they cut themselves off completely from the Mosaic religion. The Covenant of the Law ceased, once and for all, to be the state religion of Israel at the very beginning of her independent existence, in the reign of her first king Jeroboam, the son of Nebat, who made Israel to sin. The Mosaic Covenant and Ordinances, which had been the religion of the chosen race up to that time, thenceforward remained the religion of the southern section only of that race, i.e. of Judah, with the result that it has in later times become customary to speak of the religion of the chosen race as "Judaism."

As a nation Israel never returned to their former worship even for a brief period. The state religion of the northern kingdom was the worship of the Golden Calves. How completely Israel broke away from the Covenant of the Law is perhaps not sufficiently appreciated. The people of Judah, who later were called Jews, in spite of all their backsliding, never in the same way nationally repudiated Mosaicism.

PUNISHMENT FORETOLD

It was well understood by both Israel and Judah that swift retribution and chastisement would be meted out to them if they forsook their God and served the false gods of the surrounding heathen. They knew full well the awful predictions of judgment connected with the Covenant which Jehovah made with them at Sinai in Horeb.

Foretold by Moses

Moses, the great lawgiver, and the leader of the Twelve Tribes from Egypt, had pronounced the dread curses that were to fall upon the Covenant-breakers and the disobedient. At Sinai the united nation had entered into a contract with God, a Covenant that was wholly conditional upon obedience. They had undertaken to do certain things and walk in obedience to God's laws; and God on His part was graciously pledged to perform certain things for them. This was the Mosaic Covenant. It was no part of the everlasting Abrahamic Covenant, it was no part of "the Promises made to the Fathers." The Abrahamic Covenant Promises were wholly unconditional. This "Old," Mosaic Covenant had not been made with Abraham, Isaac, and Jacob, but with their seed centuries later at Horeb.

"The Lord our God made a covenant with us in Horeb. The Lord made not this covenant with our fathers, but with us, even us, who are all of us here alive this day" (*Deuteronomy* 5:2, 3).

It was this temporary Mosaic Covenant that Israel nationally renounced. It was this Covenant that contained the severe penal clauses for disobedience and the breaking of the terms of the contract.

The great Punishment was known as that of the "Seven Times," and is recorded in *Leviticus* 26, where it is repeated four times, in verses 18, 21, 24 and 28, where God says He will punish or chasten His people "Seven Times."

This "Seven Times" remained for long ages a mysterious and unsolved measure of chastisement. It was undetermined in Old Testament times. Only in quite modern days has it been possible to gauge its precise meaning. Students of Prophecy are now agreed that it denotes a period of 2,520 years, an age-long punishment indeed!

The kingdom of Israel was the recipient of many warnings from God at the mouth of His servants the prophets.

Foretold by Hosea

The prophet Hosea, one of the earliest of the prophets, was a man of Judah, but his commission was not to the people of Judah, for it was confined to the house of Israel. He stood forth before the guilty kingdom and gave utterance to prophetic words of stupendous import to its people, wholly apart from and independently of the people of Judah. What he foretold was punishment severe indeed, and it indicated the fierce anger of God against His rebellious people. Under the three names of Jezreel, Lo-Ruhamah, Lo-Ammi, the Divine sentence upon this guilty people was declared. Its meaning in plain words was this:

1. God would cause to cease the kingdom of the house of Israel (*Hosea* 1:4).
2. God would no more have mercy upon the house of Israel (*Hosea* 1:6).
3. God would not be their God and they should not be His people (*Hosea* 1:9).

Terrible was this dread sentence that fell upon Israel of the northern kingdom, but it had no reference whatever to Judah.

Hosea, even as Moses had done, made a mysterious utterance concerning this coming punishment. He speaks of it as extending into a "Third Day."

"After two days will He revive us: in the *third* day He will raise us up, and we shall live in His sight" (*Hosea* 6:2).

These "Three Days," as did the "Seven Times," remained for long ages an unsolved measure of punishment, but in the present day the meaning of it is recognized with precision.

THE PUNISHMENT EXECUTED

The Empire of Assyria was the destined instrument for the execution of the Divine sentence upon the rebellious house of Israel.

The blow did not fall in one single overwhelming stroke, but at least in two and possibly three stages, of which the second was the death-blow to the kingdom. It did not take place at one single date but extended over a period of years. Isaiah the prophet in the opening days of this epoch, 741 BC, definitely foretold that within sixty-five years Israel should cease to be a people.

"Thus saith the Lord God ... within threescore and five years shall Ephraim be broken, that it be not a people" (*Isaiah* 7:7, 8).

The first phase of the Captivity took place in the days of the emperors Pul and Tiglath-Pileser, in 741 BC, evidently in two distinct campaigns. But grievous as these were they did not terminate the existence of the kingdom. Yet another twenty years elapsed before the end occurred. Samaria, after a siege of three years by Shalmanezer, fell in 721 BC. This is the crucial date of the Captivity Era of Israel. Since the beginning of the Captivity was not one single date but was spread over a period of years, known as the "Captivity Era," it is reasonable to conclude that the ending of the Captivity will not be a single date, but a corresponding epoch of years, or the "Terminal Era." Further, in the light of Isaiah's prophecy quoted above, it is certain that the Captivity Era could not be more than sixty-five years.

After these invasions the cities and territories of Israel were emptied of their inhabitants, and were at once filled up and repeopled by foreigners, who themselves were captives of Assyria from other regions. Thus the whole of Israel's land was populated by a foreign element, whose descendants, known as Samaritans, occupied a large proportion of it in the time of our Lord.

The captive Israelites on each occasion were taken away to Assyria and placed in the regions of Hala and Habor by the river of Gozan. This country today is more or less the region of Armenia, to the south-west of the Caspian Sea. It is in this region that Bible *history* leaves these Israelites. Bible *prophecy*, however, does not leave them there, but makes them travel far. Therefore the place where Israel was "lost" is the one place where they should not be found. The Apocrypha traces their history a stage further than the Bible does, for we learn from Esdras (II *Esdras* 13:40) that the main body of these captives migrated to a distant land called Ar-Sareth, which is in Europe, in the south-west of Russia, and is more or less represented today by the Ukraine. This is a notable fact and should not be forgotten. This migration took place while the kingdom of Judah was still in existence. It occurred about 650 BC, which, it is well to bear in mind, was some sixty or seventy years before the destruction of Jerusalem, nearly 150 years before the Jews returned to Palestine from their captivity in Babylon.

THE RESTORATION FORETOLD

We have now, very briefly but sufficiently for our purpose, considered the Foretelling and the Execution of Israel's punishment. Most of it is well known. What is not so fully appreciated is the fact that to this captive people, most of whom were then in Europe, were made by the mouth of God's prophets most gracious and magnificent promises of a future Restoration. These promises were to the captive Israelites and not to the Jewish Kingdom, nor to the later kingdomless Jews in Palestine after their return from Babylon. Many of these promises are quite wrongly applied to the Jews. The result is confusion, for, not being made to Judah, they very naturally do not fit them, nor do they depict their condition—all this to the great delight of the ungodly and the infidel, and to the surprise, confusion, and distress of the believer, who in consequence must seek for an explanation in various quite needless theories.

Many are the details foretold of this Restoration. If the prophecies concerning the Punishment were explicit, no less so were those dealing with the Restoration.

Restoration Guaranteed

Restoration was guaranteed on the word of the Living God. The prophets were fully persuaded of its future accomplishment. With one mouth they testify to the coming mercy and favour of God, to the coming Redemption of Israel nationally, and to the splendour of the recovery of this people. They were unanimous that the terrible doom pronounced upon Israel was not everlasting, but that it had a determined end.

THE TWO RESTORATIONS OF ISRAEL

At the beginning of this chapter it was suggested that the word "Restoration" might have more than one meaning. It might refer to more than one event. It is not commonly known that two distinct Restorations of the Ten Tribed Israel are spoken of in the Bible. There are to be two distinct gatherings of that nation.

"And it shall come to pass in that day, that the Lord shall set His hand again the second time to recover the remnant of His people, which shall be left, from Assyria, and from Egypt, and from Pathros, and from Cush, and from Elam, and from Shinar, and from Hamath, and from the islands of the sea. And He shall set up an ensign for the nations, and shall assemble the outcasts of Israel, and gather together the dispersed of Judah from the four corners of the earth" (*Isaiah* 11:11, 12).

It is evident that there are to be two gatherings or two Restorations. The above passage speaks of a second, the Final and Great Restoration of the two houses of Israel and Judah into the land promised to their fathers. But before this takes place there is to be a first or Prior gathering and Restoration of Israel alone. These are two, and quite distinct, propositions.

TABLE NO. II

THE RESTORATIONS OF ISRAEL AND JUDAH

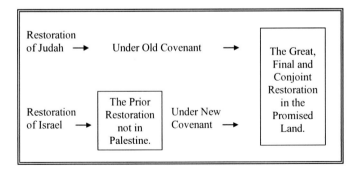

The First or Preliminary Restoration is that of Israel apart from Judah (the Jews) into some land, which is not Palestine, into which they are to come after their great dispersion and wanderings from sea to sea.

The Second or Final Restoration is the gathering of Israel of the Ten Tribes together with Judah into the Promised Land, to begin their endless occupation of it. These two Restorations need to be kept distinctly in mind and should not be confused as one single event.

Some authorities assure us that there is nothing in the Scriptures to warrant the view that there is any Restoration of Israel to blessing—

    (a)   apart from Judah, or

    (b)   apart from the land of Palestine.

Thus, one teacher writes:

"There is so much prophetic Scripture which associates the fulfilment of promised blessing to Israel with the Restoration of the Covenant-granted land, and with the reunion of the separated kingdoms of Israel and Judah, that it is justifiable inference to say that there can be no enjoyment on the part of Israel of the fulness of blessing as defined and guaranteed by Divine Counsel and declaration, except as and when the above conditions are realised."

There is indeed a mass of Scripture describing the (Final) Restoration of Israel to "fulness of blessing" associated with the Jews and with Palestine. But that is no proof that there are no passages emphasizing a Preliminary Restoration of Israel to blessings of great magnitude apart from the Jews and in some land other than Palestine. Therefore "the inference" in the above quotation is not "justifiable." References to a Final Restoration, however numerous, do not disprove or nullify definite references to a Prior Restoration. In the following pages we hope to make it clear that such a Preliminary Restoration is foretold for Israel. All are agreed as to the Final Restoration: but not all have recognized the Preliminary (and lesser if you will) Restoration which is of supreme significance in the counsel and purposes of God.

It was stated above that this Restoration of Israel was given by the prophets with a wealth of detail. By a careful study it is possible to discover the following important points—

1. The *Time* of Israel's Restoration can be definitely dated.
2. The *Place* of Israel's Restoration can be located.
3. The *Religion* of Israel's Restoration can be intimated in clear terms.
4. The *Population* of Israel at her Restoration is mentioned.

The investigation of these points will form the subject of subsequent chapters.

CHAPTER II

THE TIME OF ISRAEL'S RESTORATION

CONTENTS

THE TIME OF ISRAEL'S RESTORATION

THREE MAIN INDICATIONS

CHAPTER II

THE TIME OF ISRAEL'S RESTORATION

In the endeavour to discover the Time of Israel's Restoration and to answer the question as to when her punishment would cease, there are three lines of investigation from which information may be gained, and they are:

    i. "The Latter Days."
    ii. "The Third Day."
    iii. "The Seven Times."

Through studying these we arrive at a very remarkable period in modern history. The astonishing thing (nay, rather the most natural thing) is that the period indicated did witness the phenomenal rise of a nation and race in might, majesty, and world-dominion, the like of which has never been witnessed on this old earth of ours. This is a significant fact and merits serious consideration by every thinking man. God has verily kept His Promise and fulfilled His Word.

Israel's Restoration was to be *in* "the Latter Days," *on* "the Third Day," and *after* "the Seven Times."

i. THE LATTER DAYS

Two of the prophets speaking of Israel's Restoration mention distinctly that it was to be in "the Latter Days." What period is this? What are its limits? To answer briefly, Time in the Scriptures is divided into two main sections, which are known as "the Former Days" and "the Latter Days." The dividing point between them is the First Coming of Christ. Time before His advent is called the Former Days, and the time since that advent, right on to His Second Coming and the inauguration of the Millennium, is called the Latter Days. The Latter Days terminate with the beginning of the Millennial reign of our Lord.

We live in these Latter Days. They correspond with the Gospel Dispensation and embrace the Dispensation of the Church.

The ages BC are the Former Days, while the Latter Days are the AD age.

Jeremiah's Statement

In chapter 31 of his book Jeremiah foretold the recovery and Restoration of the house of Israel (not of Judah, the Jews of later times). In verses 1 and 2 we read:

"At the same time, saith the Lord, will I be the God of all the families of Israel, and they shall be My people. Thus saith the Lord, The people which were left of the sword found grace in the wilderness; even Israel, when I went to cause him to rest" (*Jeremiah* 31:1, 2).

Here we notice that God is about to make them His people again. After their captivity they are to "find grace," and they are "caused to rest." This is the Restoration of Israel, not the second and Final restoration, because it will be noted that it does not take place in Palestine; it is the Preliminary Restoration of Israel alone. The verse tells us that this is to happen "at the same time." What time is this? The preceding verse tells us, in "the Latter Days": it reads thus:

"The fierce anger of the Lord shall not return, until He have done it, and until He have performed the intents of His heart: *in the latter days* ye shall consider it" (*Jeremiah* 30:24).

"At the same time" "they shall be My people," they shall "find grace in the wilderness," and be "caused to rest."

The Restoration of Israel, according to Jeremiah, was to take place in "the Latter Days."

Hosea's Statement

Hosea, referring to this Restoration, spoke as follows:

"Afterward shall the children of Israel return, and seek the Lord their God, and David their king; and shall fear the Lord and His goodness *in the latter days*" (*Hosea* 3:5).

He tells of the return of the house of Israel to God; they are to seek Him and David their king and God's goodness is to be upon them. This time of favour or Restoration is to be in "the Latter Days."

This information from Jeremiah and Hosea does not carry us far in our quest. It mentions an exceedingly long period, which has already lasted 1,930 years, too extended to be of much value in answering our questions.

Concomitant Events

But the information, such as it is, is not without its value. It teaches us that the Restoration is not to be post-dated, or relegated to the millennium. It must take place before the Second Coming of our Lord and Saviour. Those who look for His immediate return should be able to point to an accomplished Restoration of the Ten Tribed kingdom of Israel.

It reminds us, moreover, that the Time of the Restoration is synchronous with the epoch in which so many of the marvellous Covenant Promises and Prophecies meet and culminate. So many wonderful predictions concerning Israel are to materialize and have their fulfilment in the Latter Days, before the millennium, that it all looks as if it were only one stupendous event or development for Israel. Thus the Time of Israel's Restoration in the Latter Days is in keeping with—

1. The Great Covenant Promises to the Fathers (*Genesis* 49:2).
2. The Predictions of Balaam's Parables (*Numbers* 24:14).
3. The Blessings pronounced by Moses (*Deuteronomy* 31:28 and 33).
4. The Development of the Fifth, Stone Empire of Nebuchadnezzar's Dream (*Daniel* 2)—

all of which were for realization in "the Latter Days."

It will of course be anticipated that "the Third Day" will fall in the period of "the Latter Days," and also that "the Seven Times" must of necessity end in "the Latter Days."

ii. THE THIRD DAY

The prophet Hosea not only informs us that the Restoration of Israel was to take place in "the Latter Days," but also that it was to be on "the Third Day." This is certainly mysterious.

"Come, and let us return unto the Lord; for He hath torn, and He will heal us; He hath smitten, and He will bind us up. After two days will He revive us: in *the third day* He will raise us up, and we shall live in His sight" (*Hosea* 6:1, 2).

Here are three days. In the first two the condition of Israel is represented as "torn" and "smitten," eloquent description of the misery of their captive state. Then, after the two days, on the Third Day comes a great change, the recovery and revival of the nation is depicted. There is the "returning unto the Lord" and the Restoration to favour and blessing, the return of the prodigal son to his Father. On the dawning of the Third Day there is to be evidence of national revival, and as the day advances Israel is to be "raised up" from her grave. The Third Day was to witness the Resurrection of Israel even as the third day witnessed the resurrection of Israel's Redeemer.

This "Third Day" may be called Israel's "Appointed Day," the long foretold Destined Day of blessing and glory, when the once dead nation should live again, and "live in His sight." What a thing to be alive unto God nationally!

And now comes the question, when is this Third Day? It obviously refers to no ordinary single day of twenty-four hours, but to some far greater period of time. Many a saint has doubtless pored over this subject and striven to discover the time which God's Spirit signified, and thus to solve the riddle. Many did doubtless calculate the period correctly, but either the event had not yet materialized at their time because they were living in an earlier age, or else they were actually living in the very centre of the developments and were too close to them to realize their import and to recognize that what was taking place before their very eyes was even the Restoration of Israel.

The only available clue as to the meaning of a "day" is in II *Peter* 3:8, where we read that—

"One day is with the Lord as a thousand years, and a thousand years as one day" (II *Peter* 3:8).

See *Psalm* 90:4. "A thousand years in Thy sight are but as yesterday."

On this interpretation these Three Days are periods of a thousand years each. After the second thousand years of captivity, and not till then, are we to perceive the first signs of reviving. At the dawn of the third thousand years, signs of life are to appear and as the day advances the rise of the nation must be manifest.

When do these Three Days of Hosea begin? From what date are we to reckon them? Obviously from the beginning of Israel's Punishment, from the "Captivity Era" of the Ten Tribed kingdom. As already noted, the beginning was not a single date, but a series of events during an epoch of not more than sixty-five years' duration. It began in 741 BC, and the crucial date was 721 BC, the latest possible date being 676 BC.

In calculating the period of Hosea's days the reckonings may be made in lunar, prophetic or solar years. Table No. III gives at a glance the times of Hosea's Three Days as reckoned in solar years from the three dates of the Captivity Era.

TABLE NO. III

HOSEA'S THREE DAYS

First Day <	begins ends	741 BC AD 260	721 BC AD 280	676 BC AD 325
Second Day <	begins ends	AD 260 AD 1260	AD 280 AD 1280	AD 325 AD 1325
Third Day begins		AD 1260	AD 1280	AD 1325

It will be seen that Hosea's Third Day began in the period AD 1260-1325, with AD 1280 as the most important date of that period.

23

If the reckoning be in Lunar and Prophetic years the corresponding dates are:

Lunar 1198, 1218, 1263.

Prophetic 1231, 1251, 1296.

The earliest possible beginning of the Third Day is 1198 (Lunar) and the latest beginning is 1325 (Solar): the epoch 1198 to 1325.

The statement that the Restoration of Israel was to be on the Third Day gives a far more precise epoch for that event than did the information that it was to occur in the Latter Days.

The Restoration could not take place till the beginning of "the Third Day." The determination of the beginning of this day enables us to strike off at least the first twelve centuries of "the Latter Days." The Restoration must be in "the Latter Days," at least after AD 1198.

Although we are narrowing down the time and getting nearer to the goal of our quest, we are still far from any precise date; for "the Third Day" is a period of a thousand years. The Restoration, however, was not to await the completion of the "Third Day," it was to begin at the close of "the Second Day" and therefore should be well established by the middle of "the Third Day." The middle of the Third Day would be about AD 1780. Thus we know the desired date within a margin of some 560 years.

As we contemplate in History the period covered by the first half of Hosea's "Third Day" (AD 1198 to 1780), we are faced with the remarkable spectacle of the rise of a nation and race in Europe. Surely this is significant? Exactly what was foretold, exactly what should be expected. All done so quietly, as if it were the most natural thing in the world, as indeed are all the works of God. Truly "the Kingdom of God cometh not with observation."

Table No. IV shows "the Latter Days" and Hosea's "Third Day" side by side for easy comparison.

TABLE NO. IV

THE LATTER DAYS AND HOSEA'S THREE DAYS

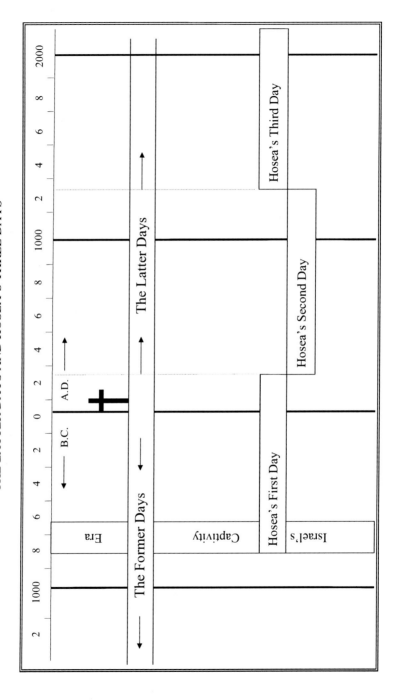

Hosea's Three Days and Ezekiel's Vision of the Dry Bones

Hosea's Three Days probably have some close connection with Ezekiel's Vision of the Valley of the Dry Bones, *Ezekiel* 37:1-14. At least there is close resemblance between them. Each deals with the house of Israel, and in each there are three stages.

Hosea's First Day corresponds exactly with the first stage of the Vision. The valley full of dry bones was eloquent of the sad picture of the scattered, hopeless and lifeless condition of Israel during the First Day. It depicted dispersion, disorder, and death.

Hosea's Second Day saw the luring and the gathering of the Tribes into the "Appointed Place." This resembled the second stage of the Vision. Where there was a shaking, the bones were sorted and gathered "bone to his bone." Order was evolved out of chaos, but it was not yet orderly *life*, "there was no life in them."

Hosea's Third Day was one of Resurrection to national life. "In the third day He will raise us up, and we shall live in His sight." So was it in the Vision. The Spirit of God breathed upon "these slain," and "the breath came into them and they lived and stood up upon their feet an exceeding great army." It was a vision of life, order, power and invincible might.

What was the sequel of the Vision? After this passing of Israel from death unto life, after this glorious Preliminary Restoration, the prophet Ezekiel tells of the still greater Restoration that was to follow, namely the Reunion of Israel with the Jews and the occupation once more by them of the Promised Land, and this under one king: "One king shall be king to them all," and "David My servant shall be king over them" (*Ezekiel* 37:15-28).

What is the history of to-day? Who has possession, not only of Palestine, but of the whole of the land promised to Abraham? The British Empire, and that under one king. His Gracious Majesty George V is to-day the ruler of Palestine. How quietly and without "observation" it all comes about! Is it not at least strange that the heir to the throne is named David, and that in the ordinary course of events David will be the next ruler of Palestine, and of the far wider territory known as the Promised Land?

Jonah's Third Day

Hosea is not the only prophet who indicates Israel's Resurrection on the Third Day. Is this not also the teaching, in type, of the prophet Jonah?

In one single particular alone was Jonah a type of our Blessed Lord.

"For as Jonas was three days and three nights in the whale's belly; so shall the Son of Man be three days and three nights in the heart of the earth" (*Matthew* 12:40).

Was not Israel's national Resurrection also foreshadowed by the same type? This prophet, save in the matter of his "burial and resurrection," was no type of our Saviour, whereas he was a very complete type of Israel, though it is not so stated in the Scriptures.

Jonah's deliberate disobedience to God, his rejection of his high calling and commission, and his running away from God were a vivid picture of the rebellious nation.

His punishment, swallowing up, and disappearance were a dramatic representation of what was to happen to Israel.

"Israel is swallowed up: now shall they be among the Gentiles as a vessel wherein is no pleasure" (*Hosea* 8:8).

Jonah's repentance, his finding grace and pardon, and his resurrection to "life" were the prophetic story of Israel, and occurred on the "Third Day."

His great Recommission and subsequent faithful work for God in the service of his fellow-men were in miniature the programme for the restored Israel of the Latter Days.

How could Israel, whom "the king of Assyria hath *devoured*" (*Jeremiah* 50:17) and who was "*swallowed up*" by the Gentile world, rise again to life on the Third Day? The marvel is all prefigured for us in the prophet Jonah. Apart from Divine interposition it is incomprehensible.

iii. THE SEVEN TIMES

We now approach the study of "the Seven Times" with increasing interest, for it is reasonable to suppose that here we shall gather information much more precise and definite. The information given as "the Latter Days" was very indefinite. Notable advance was made, however, through determining the time of Hosea's "Third Day." But that was a lengthy epoch even after it had been narrowed down within 560 years!

As already stated, Moses had foretold a "Seven Times" punishment for the breaking of the Covenant made at Sinai between God and the Twelve Tribes of Israel. What was the duration of the "Seven Times"? The information gained by students of Prophecy from already fulfilled prophecies has enabled them to determine with great assurance the value of a "time," which they considered represented 360 years. This would make the "Seven Times" the long period of 2,520 years.

We are again faced with the same question that arose in connection with the Third Day, viz., From what date are we to measure this period? Obviously, as in the previous case, the answer is, from the "Captivity Era" of Israel, the dates of which were 741, 721, and 676 BC. The starting point of "the Seven Times" is identical with that of the Three Days of Hosea.

The period may also be measured in lunar, prophetic, or solar years from each of the above dates. Table No. V gives the results.

TABLE NO. V

TERMINATIONS OF THE SEVEN TIMES PUNISHMENT

Dates of the Captivity Era of Israel	741 BC	721 BC	676 BC
Termination in Lunar Reckoning	AD 1702	AD 1722	AD 1767
Termination in Prophetic Reckoning	AD 1744	AD 1764	AD 1809
Termination in Solar Reckoning	AD 1780	AD 1800	AD 1845

The sum of the matter is that "the Seven Times" ended in the period between the extreme date AD 1702 and 1845, which is the Terminal Era of Israel's Captivity, equal to the sixty-five years of the Captivity Era plus the difference in the calculations between lunar and solar reckoning, which is seventy-five years—143 years. It is important to remember that there was no more of the Seven Times Punishment for the house of Israel after AD 1845.

The study of the termination of "the Seven Times" enables us to narrow down the Restoration period to within 140 years, between AD 1702 and 1845. Examined in the light of history, it was precisely the period, which saw the phenomenal rise of Britain. It was pre-eminently the times of her becoming "a Great and Mighty Nation" (*Genesis* 12:2 and 18:18). It was the destined day that saw the spreading abroad "to the west and to the east and to the north and to the south" (*Genesis* 28:14). Note in passing the unusual order here, "to the west" first. Did not this nation spread first to the west? Was it a mere coincidence? Ought not these things to have been so? Was it not all according to the Divine fore-ordained plan and stated purpose? This was the time of the First gathering or Preliminary Restoration of Israel. It was only after this blessedness of Israel that they could come into the occupation of the Land of Promise. Exactly so has it fallen out, for the nation has recently come into possession of Egypt, Mesopotamia, and Palestine, the exact territory the vast boundaries of which were set by the Covenant as "from the river of Egypt unto the great river, the river Euphrates" (*Genesis* 15:18), which was promised to Abraham's seed in the Latter Days.

If the Anglo-Saxon race be not Israel of the Ten Tribes, how comes it into this great inheritance just at the time that Israel should do so?

In the period under review were there any rival claimants, or any that had a vestige of title to world-supremacy as was promised to the Seed of Abraham, Isaac and Jacob? What of Spain in the sixteenth century? What of France in its Napoleonic period? What of Germany and its bid for the hegemony of the world? Every one of these great powers fully acknowledged that Britain alone was *the* real rival, and the only obstacle in the path of their ambition. To break the power of

Britain was the supreme purpose of each one. It is terribly significant, is it not, that the complete undoing of each was due to this race?

Dr. R.G. Usher, Professor of History in the Washington University, St. Louis, U.S.A., in *The Story of the Great War,* writes:

"One of the reasons why the Germans began the war was the belief that the British Empire was so weak, so disloyal, that it could not resist assault. One of the reasons why the Germans were defeated in the war was the loyalty and the strength of the British Empire. The Germans were sure that the war would create a new empire, surpassing in extent and power any of the old Empires. They were right: the war created a new British Empire, stronger, more unified than ever before, a real State, whose importance in times to come will be incalculable."

We have now investigated the subject of the *Time* of Israel's Restoration.

Table No. VI gives a summary of this chapter, and shows the relative positions of the Latter Days, Hosea's Three Days, and the Seven Times.

TABLE NO. VI

THE TIME OF ISRAEL'S RESTORATION

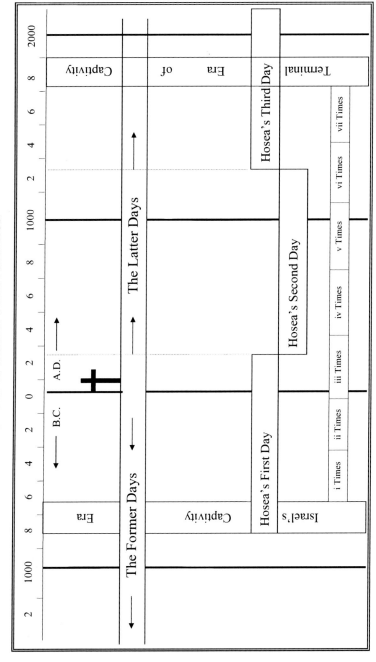

CHAPTER III

THE PLACE OF ISRAEL'S RESTORATION

CONTENTS

THE PLACE OF ISRAEL'S RESTORATION

THREE LINES OF INVESTIGATIONS

  i.   "The Appointed Place."
  ii. "The Wilderness."
  iii. "The Islands."

I.   THE "APPOINTED" PLACE
     The Promise to David.
          The Place of Safety and Restoration.
          To Israel and not to Judah.
          The Appointed Place not Palestine.
     The "Prepared Place."
          The Place of Safety.
     The Prepared Place=The Appointed Place.
     The Prepared Place=The Wilderness.

II. THE WILDERNESS
     The Place of Safety and Restoration
     Hosea ⎤
     Jeremiah ⎬ on the Wilderness
     Ezekiel ⎥
     Isaiah ⎦
     The Wilderness=The Islands.

CHAPTER III

THE PLACE OF ISRAEL'S RESTORATION

In the last chapter we found that there were data in the prophetic Scriptures regarding the *Time* of Israel's Restoration which enabled us to fix it with considerable precision. Are there data which would assist us to locate with any assurance the *Place* where it was to occur? Are there any indications of a place where the Ten Tribed captives were to be gathered; where they were to rest from their long wanderings and be secure from oppression; where they were to renew their strength and be restored to God's favour and blessing; after which they, together with the Jews, were to become the possessors of the land promised to their fathers? If this place could be located with certainty we should be justified in holding that the people who were found in the Appointed Place at the Appointed Time must be Israel.

In this search we shall proceed along three definite lines. There are allocated for Israel's Restoration three regions. These, it might be expected, all refer to one and the same place or country. Thus there is reference to—

   i.   An *Appointed Place* for Israel.
   ii. Some *Wilderness* for Israel.
  iii. Certain *Islands* for Israel.

This land or country was one that was definitely appointed for them by God. God Himself was to draw them thither. It was a place of Isolation and Safety, a Strong Defensive Position, a Place of great Fertility and Abundance, of Temporal and Spiritual Blessings. In fact, it was a goodly heritage.

i. THE APPOINTED PLACE

When God made His great Covenant with David His servant relating to the perpetuity of His dynasty, He at the same time coupled it with the somewhat mysterious promise of a Place for Israel—a prophecy that has attracted but little attention. This Dual Promise is found in II *Samuel* 7. There is doubtless a close and intimate connection between the two sections of it, and they are mutually interdependent. What exactly was the promise of this Place?

> "Moreover I will *appoint a place* for My people Israel,
> and will plant them,
> that they may dwell in a place of their own,
> and move no more;
> neither shall the children of wickedness afflict them any more, as beforetime" (II *Samuel* 7:10).

Note well the terms of the promise. Here we have the "Appointed Place." God Himself would select this place, and He Himself would plant Israel there. It would be a place prepared for them, and set apart for the nation of the Ten Tribes and not for the house of Judah, the Jews. "Israel" here does not mean the whole of the Twelve Tribes, for the following two reasons:—

1. Though, at the time when this striking promise was given, the Twelve Tribes were united and formed a single people and kingdom under the rule of David, yet it was a time when the distinction between Israel and Judah was very marked. In the reigns of Saul and David the difference is constantly emphasized. The division of the Twelve Tribes into the two nations of Israel and Judah after the death of Solomon was only the confirmation of a very real cleavage that had already existed at least for more than a century and a quarter. Hence, when the verse says "Israel," we take it to mean Israel in contradistinction to Judah.

2. The second reason is that the blessing here promised has never fallen to the lot of the Jews. They have never had any place of their own other than Palestine. They have never had a settled abode or permanent home. Their experience has never been a "planting," but on the contrary a constantly recurring uprooting. Instead of freedom from oppression, affliction and persecution have been the sad lot of their inheritance; whereas it can be shown that to Israel the items of this promise have been fulfilled to the very letter.

The Appointed Place not Palestine

This Appointed Place is not Palestine. It is some other good land, an additional territory for Israel.

1. It could hardly be Palestine because that land had already been appointed by Oath and Covenant to all the Twelve Tribes many centuries before David's time. This promise is no reiteration of the old one. At this very period the people were in the secure occupation of the land promised to their Fathers. It would be strange to promise it now when it had already been promised long ago, and when it was actually in their possession.

2. It could hardly be Palestine because once they were in possession of this Appointed Place they were never to be ousted. They were to "move no more," according to the words of the promise. Whereas the Jews were certainly evicted from Palestine in AD 70.

3. It could hardly be Palestine because that country was never the isolated and strongly defensive position which the Appointed Place was to be, for Palestine was peculiarly open and liable to attack from north and south. If it were not actually the cockpit of the old heathen Empires, it was the pathway of their armies. The Appointed Place is clearly not Palestine.

It may come as a surprise to many to learn from Scripture that Israel was to have any home other than the Land promised to their Fathers. Yet such is the promise; for it is no temporary shelter, but a permanent home given to them in addition to the Promised Land.

The promise implied impending affliction at the hand of their enemies, but definitely states the appointment of a Place of ultimate rest and safety. Here is a Place of Recovery, a Place for the Restoration of the Ten Tribes. There is no hint, however, in the promise of the whereabouts of this goodly heritage. The Appointed Place is not every place to which Israel eventually was to spread abroad, but was a very definite single country from which expansion was to take place.

In concluding this section on the "Appointed Place" attention should be given to the mention in the book of The Revelation of a similar place that is spoken of as a "Prepared Place."

The Prepared Place

In chapter 12 of The Revelation the Apostle had seen "a great wonder," "a woman clothed with the sun, and the moon under her feet, and upon her head a crown of twelve stars." She was delivered of a man child, and there appeared another wonder, "a great red dragon" ready to devour the newborn. But the child was caught up to God in heaven, and the woman fled from the dragon.

> "And the woman fled into *the wilderness*, where she hath a *Place Prepared* of God, that they should feed her there a thousand, two hundred and threescore days" (*Revelation* 12:6).

Who is this woman? Does she represent Israel? Many think she does, and so it may be. It would then seem more than likely that the "Appointed Place" was this "Prepared Place."

It is clear that the Prepared Place is to be a place of safety and protection for the afflicted, just as was the Appointed Place. In this place the woman was to be defended from the face of "the serpent," and be free from affliction and persecution (verse 13), and there she was to be nourished. It reads very like the Appointed Place save that it is not stated to be a perpetual home, but one for only a period equivalent to half a "Seven Times," 1,260 years.

In the 14th verse of that chapter it states:

> "And to the woman were given two wings of a great eagle, that she might fly into the *wilderness*, into *her place*, where she is nourished for a time, and times, and half a time, from the face of the serpent" (*Revelation* 12:14).

Here we have the Place mentioned again. In both the verses it is stated that the woman fled to the "Wilderness." The "Prepared Place" is some "Wilderness." This is an important clue. The "Wilderness" will merit careful examination.

ii. "THE WILDERNESS"

The Restoration of Israel in some certain place, prior to the great Final Restoration with the Jews to the possession of the Land promised to the Fathers, is described by at least four of the leading prophets. They all describe it as a resting place or a sanctuary, where the tribes were to renew their strength. A place of complete safety. A very rich and fertile land. A land in which there was to be abundant spiritual blessing.

The singular point is that these four prophets, who are enthusiastic over this region, speak of it as a "Wilderness," exactly as the "Prepared Place" is described by St. John as "the Wilderness." These prophets are Hosea, Isaiah, Jeremiah, and Ezekiel.

Since the word "wilderness" in the Scriptures is sometimes used to denote a place of desolation and woe and a region of punishment, we are very apt to think that it must always be a place more or less dreadful and an arid desert. This is far from being the case. From the descriptions given by these prophets it is evident that it is no desert or arid land, but on the contrary one of exceeding fertility and fruitfulness, so that by the term "wilderness" must be understood a country uninhabited and unknown, of virgin forests and undulating plains, of hills and valleys, of streams and rivers, such as these islands of ours were in the days of the early settlers.

(a) **Hosea on the Wilderness**

Hosea's mission was entirely to the house of Israel and the whole of his book deals with the people of the northern kingdom and not with the people of Judah, except in those verses in which Judah is either named or clearly indicated. He prophesied fifty years before the captivity of Israel began (two full centuries before the destruction of Judah). In Hosea's time Judah was more or less walking with God, whereas Israel had hopelessly lapsed from His worship. He stated that whereas God would not have mercy on Israel He would have mercy upon Judah (*Hosea* 1:7).

It has already been noticed that the judgments pronounced on Israel by Hosea were very terrible. Yet no prophet foretells a Restoration with such confidence or describes it so enthusiastically. In his second chapter he describes first the punishment, and then what God will do in the way of mercy and forgiveness to His rebellious people.

"Therefore, behold, I will allure her, and bring her into *the wilderness*, and speak comfortably unto her" (*Hosea* 2:14).

The place of assembly of the wanderers is "the Wilderness." It is clearly a region predetermined of God. He draws the Tribes to that trysting-place. Beautiful is the description of the gathering: "I will allure her and bring her into the wilderness." It is a place of isolation suitable for safety and recuperation, a land of joy and abundance. In this Wilderness, and not in Palestine, God was to "betroth" Israel unto Himself. There can be no doubt that this region is not Palestine. It is surely "the Appointed Place." It is surely the same "Wilderness" which was "the Prepared Place." Thus we learn from Hosea that there is to be a Restoration of Israel, apart from Judah, and in some "Wilderness," prior to their reunion and Final Restoration to the possession of the Promised Land (see *Hosea* 1:10 and 11).

(b) **Jeremiah on "the Wilderness"**

Jeremiah the prophet lived in the period that followed the downfall of the kingdom of Israel and the deportation of that nation to Assyria and after their migration thence into Europe. He lived in the days of the decadence and fall of the kingdom of Judah. Some of his prophecies solely concern and refer to the already captive Israel, while others refer and are addressed only to the Jews. He not only foretold but also witnessed the downfall of Judah.

Speaking of Israel in captivity, he made the following declaration, in which he told of their Restoration as taking place in "the Wilderness" even as Hosea did.

"At the same time, saith the Lord, will I be the God of all the families of Israel, and they shall be My people. Thus saith the Lord, the people which were left of the sword found grace in *the wilderness*; even Israel, when I went to cause him to rest" (*Jeremiah* 31:1, 2).

Here is this "Wilderness" mentioned again by a second prophet in connection with the Restoration of Israel. The *Time* of this occurrence has already been discussed. They that were left of the sword, even Israel, after their Assyrian captivity were to foregather in "the Wilderness" for the purpose of resting. God Himself "went" to do this. He was the Director of the great movement into this prearranged place. There was some mysterious lure in this "Wilderness" for the Tribes of Israel. Behind all the apparent aimlessness of their wanderings was the Divine purpose. God was drawing them with the cords of love.

Jeremiah's description of "the Wilderness" entirely corroborates that of Hosea. Both prophets describe the same place and the same event. This Restoration is not the Final Restoration of the Twelve Tribes, it has no connection with Palestine or with the Jews. The first half of *Jeremiah* 31 refers only to Israel of the Ten Tribes.

So far there has been no indication as to where this land lies, though it is obviously the same "Wilderness" that is mentioned in The Revelation.

(c) Ezekiel on "the Wilderness"

Ezekiel prophesied some 130 years after the kingdom of Israel had ceased to exist. He was carried captive to Babylon in the second deportation of the Jews, which was in the reign of Jehoiachin, some seven years after Daniel had been taken away, and some twelve years before the destruction of Jerusalem. When speaking of Israel's Restoration, Ezekiel mentions "the Wilderness" as the place where God would deal graciously with them and bless them. Thus we have a third prophet who speaks of Israel's place of Restoration as "the Wilderness." He calls it "the Wilderness of the people":

"As I live, saith the Lord God, surely with a mighty hand, and with a stretched out arm, and with fury poured out, will I rule over you: And I will bring you out from the people, and will gather you out of the countries wherein ye are scattered, with a mighty hand, and with a stretched out arm, and with fury poured out. And I will bring you into *the Wilderness* of the people, and there will I plead with you face to face.... And I will cause you to pass under the rod, and will bring you into the Bond of the Covenant" (*Ezekiel* 20:33-37).

Israel does not come into this region by chance or accident. It is the God-prearranged rallying-point for the race—"I will bring you... and will gather you," very like the "planting" in the Appointed Place, and like the "luring" into the Wilderness. They were gathered and brought into it after the fury of God had been poured out upon them in chastisement, after their scattering, and after their long wanderings. It is a place of rest and quietness, where God is able to plead with them. It was a place apart and separate from other peoples. It was to be a place of great spiritual blessing even as "the Wilderness" was in the descriptions of Hosea and Jeremiah.

This gathering of the Tribes to the God-appointed rendezvous is shown by the context of the above quotation to be prior to the return to the land promised to their Fathers. It was the Preliminary Restoration of the house of Israel and not the great and Final Restoration. The gathering into "the Wilderness of the people" was to take place before entering into the occupation of "the land of Israel, into the country for which I lifted up Mine hand to give it to your fathers" (*Ezekiel* 20:42).

Of the whereabouts of this "Wilderness" Ezekiel gives us no information. It is clear that it is the same Wilderness spoken of by Hosea and Jeremiah. It is impossible to prove that it is not "the Appointed Place" and "the Prepared Place." The teaching of Scripture that there is to be a Preliminary Restoration of Israel is very manifest.

(d) Isaiah on "the Wilderness"

Isaiah is yet another, the fourth, prophet who describes the Restoration of Israel as taking place in "the Wilderness." He lived and prophesied before the time of Jeremiah or of Ezekiel. The kingdom of Israel in his day was at the worst and last stage of its existence. But it was otherwise with Judah. Judah continued as a realm for a century after the time of Isaiah.

"Sing unto the Lord a new song, and His praise from the end of the earth, ye that go down to the sea, and all that is therein: the isles, and the inhabitants thereof. Let *the wilderness* and the cities thereof lift up their voice, the villages that Kedar doth inhabit: let the inhabitants of the rock sing, let them shout from the top of the mountains. Let them give glory unto the Lord, and declare His praise in *the islands*" (*Isaiah* 42:10-12).

This "Wilderness" is to be a place of joy and gladness, of rich spiritual blessing. It is in marked contrast with captivity, oppression, and wanderings. Moreover, it is a place to which God has brought His people (see verse 16).

"I will bring the blind by a way that they knew not; and I will lead them in paths that they have not known: and I will make darkness light before them, and crooked things straight. These things will I do unto them, and not forsake them" (*Isaiah* 42:16).

The "Wilderness" is the destined rendezvous of the nation. Its description entirely precludes it from the possibility of being Palestine. Isaiah's words were addressed here to the captives of the House of Israel. Isaiah's "Wilderness" is surely "the Appointed" and "the Prepared Place."

In our investigation up to this point there has been no hint as to where this wilderness is located, but in the verses above we have the first clue, the association of "the Wilderness" with "Isles" and "Islands." This is most important, and brings us to the third and last stage of our search for the Place of the Restoration.

CHAPTER IV

THE PLACE OF ISRAEL'S RESTORATION
(*continued*)

CONTENTS

CHAPTER IV

THE PLACE OF ISRAEL'S RESTORATION (*Contd.*)

Thus far in the search for this good land we arrived at certain conclusions:

1. That God had appointed some special place for Israel outside Palestine, whither the nation was to come after great affliction and wandering.

2. That there was also a "Prepared Place" for the protection and sustenance of the persecuted Woman, who is supposed to represent Israel.

3. That this "Prepared Place" was some "Wilderness."

4. That four Prophets spoke of the Restoration of Israel as occurring in "the Wilderness."

5. That a clue was given that "the Wilderness" was certain "Isles" or "Islands."

In the present chapter this clue will be followed up. It will be found that not only do the prophets describe the restoration of Israel to God's blessing and favour in "the Wilderness," but that two of them describe it as taking place in "Islands." Are they identical places? It is exceedingly improbable that there are to be two separate places for this resurrection of the race. They are surely the same region. They cannot be Palestine, since "Islands" cannot be taken to describe that land.

To quote once again those verses from Isaiah which associate "the Wilderness" with "Islands":

"Sing unto the Lord a new song, and His praise from the end of the earth, ye that go down to the sea, and all that is therein: *the isles*, and the inhabitants thereof. Let *the wilderness* and the cities thereof lift up their voice, the villages that Kedar doth inhabit: let the inhabitants of the rock sing, let them shout from the top of the mountains. Let them give glory unto the Lord, and declare His praise in *the Islands*" (*Isaiah* 42:10-12).

Isaiah thus associates "the Wilderness" with "Islands," not with any single island, but with a group of Isles. "The Wilderness" and "the Islands" here seem to be interchangeable terms and to refer to the same country. It has been already mentioned that "the Wilderness" was a place of spiritual blessing, and here the same is the case with "the Isles."

Isaiah is not the only prophet who associates "the Wilderness" with "Islands." Jeremiah also emphasizes the same connection. In the beautiful thirty-first chapter, which is mainly devoted to Israel (verses 5, 6, 9, 18, and 20), and in which the distinction between Israel and Judah is very marked, there is the mention of "the Wilderness" in the second verse and "the Isles" in the tenth. Both verses refer to the same gracious Restoration of Israel. For convenience of comparison both verses are subjoined:

"Thus saith the Lord, The people which were left of the sword found grace in *the wilderness;* even Israel, when I went to cause him to rest" (*Jeremiah* 31:2). ...

"Hear the word of the Lord, O ye nations, and declare it in *the Isles* afar off, and say, He that scattered Israel will gather him, and keep him, as a shepherd doth his flock. For the Lord hath redeemed Jacob, and ransomed him from the hand of him that was stronger than he" (*Jeremiah* 31:10, 11).

Just as "the Wilderness," so were "the Isles" to be a place of sanctuary whither the Lord was to "gather" the tribes, a place of safety and protection from affliction, and a land of rest and recovery after wanderings. The great national regeneration was to be effected in "the Wilderness," otherwise in "the Isles."

That this message by Jeremiah referred to the Ten Tribed people is shown by the preceding verse, 9:

"They shall come with weeping, and with supplications will I lead them; I will cause them to walk by the rivers of waters in a straight way, wherein they shall not stumble: for I am a father to Israel and Ephraim is My firstborn" (*Jeremiah* 31:9).

There is no reference here to the Jews.

It is not a little surprising to most people to learn that Israel was to be restored in Islands, but such indeed is the teaching of Jeremiah and more especially of Isaiah. References to Israel in the Islands by this latter prophet are truly striking.

In all its long history the Jewish section of God's chosen race was never associated with "Islands." The Jews have never lived in "the Islands." They have never been "gathered" into them and been "kept" there by God "as a shepherd doth his flock." They have never been a maritime people. But such has been the experience of Israel. The cessation of the Seven Times punishment for the house of Judah must take place years after that of the house of Israel; because their punishment began 130 years after that of Israel. As we have endeavoured to show, Israel's punishment ceased many years ago, whereas that of the Jews is only now drawing to a close. Though near the end, they are still in the terminal era of their captivity.

Isaiah and Jeremiah certainly give us to understand that there is a Restoration of Israel in "the Islands." It is abundantly clear, therefore, that there is such a thing as a Preliminary Restoration of the Ten Tribes to the favour of God, not associated with Palestine and not associated with the Jews.

Do Isaiah and Jeremiah give any indications as to where these Islands are? Are they the Ægean Islands, or Cyprus, Crete, Sicily, Sardinia, or Corsica in the Mediterranean Sea? Or are they the still further off British Islands, on the outermost part of Europe? These latter were the furthest off of all from Palestine, lying in a due north-westerly direction. They were on the outermost edge of the European continent, the veritable end of the then known earth. Nothing further west was known, all beyond being a blank.

In the first place more than one island is indicated, the plural being always used in the prophecies. This fact alone would rule out all single islands, such as we have mentioned. It has been contended that the word "Islands" in the Hebrew may be read as "coastlands" or "seacoasts." Even if this were so, how else could the prophet possibly indicate "Islands?" This would be his only way of doing it; and in such a case the word would refer to the outer coastlands of Europe including, if not coinciding with, the outermost islands. But it has been pointed out that there are no less than nine Hebrew words to express "Coastlands," while there is but *one* meaning "Islands," and this is the word used by the prophets and so translated in our Bible.

THE SUITABLILITY OF THESE VARIOUS ISLANDS

The consideration of the suitability of the British Isles to meet the requirements of the prophecies descriptive of Israel's Restoration will emphatically demonstrate that they are the only one possible group that could do so. Thus, are any of these Islands, except the British Isles, of a size capable of sustaining a teeming population or of providing a suitable home for a world power, and for a great and mighty nation? Do any of them, save the British Isles, afford a suitable base for vast colonial expansion? Could any of them provide a sanctuary from affliction at the hand of foes? Do any of them, save the British Isles, constitute a strong, defensive position where the people might "dwell in safety alone"? (*Deuteronomy* 33:28). Have any of them, save the British Isles, ever experienced the mighty spiritual blessings that were to fall upon Israel in "the Wilderness" and "the Islands"?

THE HISTORY OF THE VARIOUS ISLANDS

As one thinks over the histories of these various islands, were there ever any gatherings of immigrant peoples on those shores that might be construed as the assembling of the Tribes of Israel, with a subsequent development into a great and mighty nation and the very fullness of the nations? Has anything ever occurred in any of them resembling the Restoration or Resurrection of a race? To be more precise, bearing in mind the exact epoch of Israel's Restoration, did any event occur in any of them during that epoch which could approximately be considered as Israel's Restoration? History answers that only in the British Isles has such an event been witnessed. History corroborates Reason, and both confirm Prophecy.

To return again to the verses already quoted from Isaiah (42:10-12), and Jeremiah (31:2 and 10). Is there any indication as to where these "islands" are?

To take *Isaiah* 42:10-12: the praises of God are to arise from Israel, a maritime people, who live in "the isles," and it is said that these praises arise from "*the end of the earth*," not from the *ends* of the earth, not from the four quarters of the globe, but from *the end* of the earth, *the end* of the then known land. This is decidedly suggestive. What islands were at *the end* of the then known world? This description excludes all the islands in the Mediterranean Sea.

Or again in *Jeremiah* 31:10: the word of the Lord is to be declared "in the isles *afar off.*" Which are the islands "afar off" from Palestine? Surely not those in the Mediterranean? The British Isles were the only really far-off isles. Thus do Isaiah and Jeremiah point unmistakably to the same quarter and to the same group.

It has already been said that the references by Isaiah to islands were remarkable in character and not few in number.

Isaiah 41:1 shows that "the islands" were to be a place of much blessing and of Restoration.

"Keep silence before Me, O islands; and let the people renew their strength" (*Isaiah* 41:1).

The same thing is predicted to take place in the "islands" as was foretold should occur in "the wilderness." Israel was to rest and recover her strength. This verse cannot refer to the Jews, since the Jews have never been restored in islands. Their Restoration can only take place in Palestine through the instrumentality of Israel.

Once again Isaiah (in chapter 24) prophesied that the praises of God are to be heard from the sea and from "*the isles of the sea,*" and that those in "the isles" are to glorify the name of the Lord God of Israel.

"They shall lift up their voice, they shall sing for the majesty of the Lord, they shall cry aloud from the sea. Wherefore glorify ye the Lord in the fires, even the name of the Lord God of Israel in *the isles of the sea.* From the *uttermost part of the earth* have we heard songs, even glory to the righteous" (*Isaiah* 24:14-16).

These songs and praises from the sea and from the isles of the sea are "from the *uttermost part* of the earth," not the uttermost *parts* of the earth, but, as we have noticed before, from *the end* of the earth. What islands were at the "uttermost part of the earth"? Not those in the Mediterranean, but the British Isles alone.

Before leaving this expression, "uttermost part of the earth," it may be mentioned that it occurs in a remarkable passage referring to the kingdom of Israel in the New Testament.

Before our Blessed Lord's Ascension the disciples asked Him if He would at that time restore the kingdom to Israel.

"When they therefore were come together, they asked of Him, saying, Lord, wilt Thou at this time restore again the kingdom to Israel?" (*Acts* 1:6).

Our Lord replied that it was not for them to know the times and seasons, which God kept in His own power.

"And He said unto them, It is not for you to know the times or the seasons, which the Father hath put in His own power. But ye shall receive power, after that the Holy Ghost is come upon you; and ye shall be witnesses unto Me both in Jerusalem, and in all Judea, and in Samaria, and unto *the uttermost part of the earth*" (*Acts* 1:7, 8).

Our Lord did not tell them that they were wrong or that they had mistaken ideas of the Kingdom of Israel. On the contrary, He implies that they were right, but that the time for the revelation had not yet come. Having told them that it was not to be made known to them, He gave them this great consolation, namely, that they should be fitted to be His witnesses in Jerusalem, Judea, Samaria, and *the uttermost part of the earth*. This is invariably interpreted as the uttermost *parts* of the earth, and the same thing as preaching His name among the nations (*Luke* 24:47), or as "Go ye into all the world, and preach the Gospel to every creature" (*Mark* 16:15). The fact, however, remains that on this particular occasion, when speaking of the Kingdom of Israel, our Lord referred specially to *the uttermost part of the earth*.

To revert to *Isaiah* 24:14 quoted above, the verse speaks of "*the isles of the sea*." Now there are no islands save those of the seas. The expression is a redundancy. One single word in the Hebrew language stands for both "sea" and for "west." It would therefore be correct to render the phrase, "the islands of the *west*," which helps to confirm all the previous indications of their identification. The islands of the west, those at "the end of the earth," and those at "the uttermost part of the earth" are all one and the same group.

These "islands of the west" are again mentioned as "the islands of the sea" in *Isaiah* 11:11:

"And it shall come to pass in that day, that the Lord shall set His hand again the second time to recover the remnant of His people, which shall be left, from Assyria, and from Egypt, and from Pathros, and from Cush, and from Elam, and from Shinar, and from Hamath and from *the islands of the sea.* And He shall set up an ensign for the nations, and shall assemble the outcasts of Israel, and the dispersed of Judah from the four corners of the earth" (*Isaiah* 11:11, 12).

Here we have reference to the second or Final Restoration of the two nations of Israel and the Jews to the possession of Palestine, and amongst the various places from whence they gather are "the islands of the west."

"Behold, these shall come *from far*: and, lo, these from *the north and from the west*: and these from the land of Sinim" (*Isaiah* 49:12).

These people of God are to come "from far," which, as already seen, was a description of the position of "the islands" where Israel was to dwell. In this verse we are told that this *far* place is *the north and the west*, which is the Hebrew expression for "north-west." What place might this be? It will be noticed that the chapter begins with an instruction to Israel in "the isles":

"Listen, O *isles*, unto Me; and ye people *from far*" (*Isaiah* 49:1).

These "isles" and these people are described as "from far." These are the people who return, as stated above in verse 12, "from far," and from "the north-west." Is it not clear that these "isles" are those of the far north-west and that the British Isles alone answer to the description of far north-west from Palestine?

Is it not remarkable that the people living in the British Isles did rise to might and power as the premier nation of the world in the very epoch in which Israel's Restoration was due?

Further, is it not remarkable that, after this Resurrection of the nation in the isles, she has now entered into the possession of the Land promised to the fathers?—that they should have gone there from what used to be "the end of the earth" or "the uttermost part of the earth," even from "the islands of the west," even from the far "north-west"? Everything is exactly as foretold, and coming to pass as if it were the most natural thing in the world. Yea, so easily and quietly is God's word being fulfilled that men do not perceive it.

Isaiah refers once again to "isles" with reference to the Final Restoration:

"Surely *the isles* shall wait for Me, and the ships of Tarshish first, to bring thy sons *from far*, their silver and their gold with them, unto the name of the Lord thy God, and to the Holy One of Israel, because He hath glorified thee" (*Isaiah* 60:9).

Here again we have "the islands"; the isles and the ships of Tarshish; it is they who, under God, effect the Final Restoration of Israel and Judah. The isles cannot be other than those previously described and located by the prophet, which, even as these are, were said to be "from far." The ships of Tarshish belong to the "isles of Tarshish," the British Isles. It is clear that before the Final Restoration of Israel and the Jews to the Land of Promise there must be this Prior or Preliminary Restoration of Israel in the islands. The evidence for this seems overwhelming.

This concludes our study of Isaiah on "the isles." Jeremiah has at least one other reference to the British Isles which may be noticed, though its bearing on the Restoration may be nil. The prophet was commissioned by God to warn certain nations and kingdoms that they should drink of the cup of His fury, and amongst the number are found the kings of "the isles, which are *beyond the sea*" (*Jeremiah* 25:22). The sea here mentioned is the Mediterranean, so the islands were those beyond the Mediterranean Sea. These could only be the British Isles. It is interesting to note that these islands of ours were definitely within the scope of the prophet's great commission—Irish tradition assures us that he did actually come to these isles.

All the evidence that exists as to the whereabouts of these islands points solely to the British Isles, and there is none to the contrary.

Our investigations concerning the *Place* of the Restoration have led, then, to the following conclusions:

The Appointed Place	.	.	= The Prepared Place.
The Prepared Place.	.	.	= The Wilderness.
The Wilderness	.	.	= The Islands.
The Islands . .	.	.	= The British Isles.

The only logical conclusion is that the Anglo-Saxon race can be none other than the house of Israel. The study of the *Time* of the Restoration led to the same conclusion.

It may be asked, When and how did the Tribes arrive in this Appointed Place? Obviously they should be there before the earliest dawn of Hosea's Third Day, i.e. before 1198. What was the history of our Island before this important epoch? (See Table No.VII).

Early in the Second Day this "Wilderness" or "Island" was absolutely vacated by the Romans of their own free will (AD 410). They were not driven out, they simply evacuated this island contrary to the desires of the inhabitants. The God of Israel caused them to move away to make room for the advent of Israel to the Appointed Place. After the end of the Roman occupation it became the scene of continuous raids, invasions, and settlements by fierce tribes from across the North Sea. From the middle of the fifth century onwards until 1066 the luring into the "Wilderness" went on and was complete before the dawn of the Third Day (see Table No. VII). One race, all descended from one stock, under the various names of Jutes, Angles, Saxons, Danes, and Normans, had invaded these shores and settled in these islands to form the English nation. They united with the Britons, Kymri, Celts, Scots, and Picts, who were here before them, and formed the British race. It was from this "Appointed Place" and from this consolidated people that there sprang the great Anglo-Saxon nations of to-day, viz. the United States of America, the Dominion of Canada, the Commonwealth of Australia, the Dominion of New Zealand, and the Union of South Africa.

Thus history finds this people in "the Appointed Place" at "the Appointed Time" fulfilling "the Appointed Destiny" of Israel.

TABLE NO. VII

BRITAIN IN HOSEA'S SECOND DAY

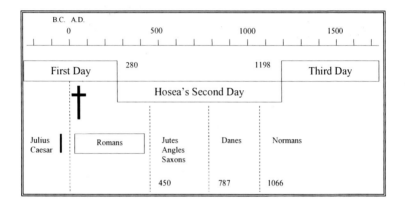

CHAPTER V

THE RELIGION OF ISRAEL'S RESTORATION

CONTENTS

CHAPTER V

THE RELIGION OF ISRAEL'S RESTORATION

When the Ten Tribes of Israel were carried away captive they were an aggressively idolatrous people. In their captivity they were to be "joined to idols." When assembling in "the Islands" they were to be a heathen people. When lured into "the Wilderness" they were still to be idolaters (*Hosea* 2:13, 14).

What was to be their religion when they were to be restored to the favour of God in this "Wilderness," "Appointed Place," or "Islands"? Is there any light on this important point in the prophecies? Was Israel to be:—

1. An idolatrous people as they were when they were led away captive into Assyria? Or—
2. A people once again under the Mosaic Covenant? Or—
3. A Christian nation under the New Covenant?

It is inconceivable that when restored to favour they would remain heathen. Were they to return and re-enter the Old Mosaic Covenant? Could such a thing be possible? The Bible is not silent upon this point but gives precise and definite information on the subject.

One often has heard the statement that Israel is to return to Palestine in unbelief, that is, under the Mosaic Covenant, and not as believers in our Lord Jesus Christ. The statement is most misleading and incorrect. If the expression is limited to the Jewish people (the Judah branch of the chosen seed of Abraham, Isaac, and Jacob) it is absolutely true. But if it is intended to include the Israel of the Ten Tribes it is absolutely untrue, as will be discovered by careful investigation. To anticipate the result of our research. When the Final Restoration of Israel and the Jews to the possession of the Promised Land takes place, the Jews will return in unbelief, under the Old Mosaic Covenant, whereas Israel will return as a nationally Christian people under the New Covenant. At their Preliminary Restoration in the islands Israel, as will presently be seen, will have come into the New Covenant and be nationally a Christian people, and as such will be restored with their brethren the Jews, who will be still under the Old Covenant, to the possession of the Land of Promise.

The descriptions of Israel's Restoration by the five prophets Hosea, Isaiah, Jeremiah, Ezekiel, and Zechariah are explicit on this topic. During the study of the Place and Time of the Restoration several verses were examined; they will now be found to contain some points bearing on the question.

I. HOSEA'S PREDICTIONS

(i) **Hosea's First Chapter**

After foretelling in its earlier verses the dire judgment on the Ten Tribed Kingdom, this first chapter passes on in verse 10 to tell of its great recovery and its Restoration to favour and blessing:

"Yet the number of the children of Israel shall be as the sand of the sea, which cannot be measured nor numbered: and it shall come to pass, that in the place where it was said unto them, Ye are not My people, there it shall be said unto them, Ye are the sons of the Living God" (*Hosea* 1:10).

The reference here is not to Judah at all, but solely to Israel. Israel is to be:

1. an innumerable host, and
2. "the Sons of the Living God."

In the following verse we read that Israel and Judah are thereupon to be gathered together and come up out of that land:

"Then shall the children of Judah and the children of Israel be gathered together, and appoint themselves one head, and they shall come up out of the land; for great shall be the day of Jezreel" (*Hosea* 1:11).

Here is the great and Final Restoration of Israel and Judah, evidently to the Promised Land. Israel and Judah are to be gathered together and "come up out of" some land under a single leader or sovereign head. Out of what land? Some land of blessing which is not Palestine. Is it not the Appointed Place? From these verses two things are clear, namely that when Israel and Judah unite under one leadership, Israel is to be a teeming population which is to be called "the Sons of the Living God." These blessings have been bestowed on Israel not in association with the house of Judah and not in association with the Land of Promise. It is as the "Sons of the Living God" that Israel is to be joined by the Jews in the possession of the Promised Land. From other scriptures we learn that the Jews are to return to Palestine in unbelief and that they will be converted to their Messiah there. But Israel will become "the Sons of the Living God" in some other land.

The expression "the Sons of the Living God" signifies being under the New Covenant in Christ Jesus, and implies being a Christian nation. Hosea's teaching is clear that Israel must be a Christian people before possessing Palestine and before the reunion with Judah.

(ii) Hosea's Second Chapter

In Chapter 2 we have:
1. verses 1-6, a description of Israel's wickedness and unfaithfulness to God through her idolatries;
2. verses 7-13, a description of severe punishment; and
3. verses 14 to end, the account of her redemption and Restoration. Verse 14 tells of her being brought into "the Wilderness."

"Therefore, behold, I will allure her, and bring her into *the wilderness*, and speak comfortably unto her" (*Hosea* 2:14).

This Wilderness is not Palestine and this Restoration cannot be the Final one. The Jews are not associated with the Ten Tribes here. Does not the "speaking comfortably" imply spiritual blessing?—the blessings of the Gospel? What do verses 19 and 20 signify?

"And I will betroth thee unto Me forever; yea, I will betroth thee unto Me in righteousness, and in judgment, and in lovingkindness, and in mercies. I will even betroth thee unto Me in faithfulness; and thou shalt know the Lord" (*Hosea* 2:19, 20).

Israel's remarriage to God, her betrothal, means that she will be brought into Covenant union with God. Would this be under the old marriage bond, or a new bond, under the New Covenant? It cannot be the old bond because this betrothal is everlasting, it is to be *"for ever"*—"I will betroth thee unto Me for ever." Not in Palestine, but previous to that, in "the Wilderness," is Israel to become a Christian nation.

It will be observed that it is after this betrothal that God would "sow her unto Him in the earth" (verse 23). Only after her union with God is Israel to enter upon her colonial expansion and be sown in the earth; and this not a punitive scattering, but a spreading abroad, as long before predicted (*Genesis* 28:14), a spreading abroad to the west and to the east, and to the north and to the south, in honour and power.

Is not all this the literal history of the Anglo-Saxon race? Was not this people lured and brought into this "Wilderness," these "islands," and nationally betrothed to God? Was it not after this that their colonial expansion began? Was it not subsequently that they entered, with the other section of the chosen seed of Abraham, the Jews, into the possession of the Land of Promise?

(iii) Hosea's Third Chapter

In the fifth verse of the third chapter, we read:

"Afterward shall the children of Israel return, and seek the Lord their God; and David their king: and shall fear the Lord and His goodness in the latter days" (*Hosea* 3:5).

The time of Israel's conversion is to be in "the latter days," that is before the Millennium, but Judah is to turn to the Messiah when He returns the second time. His glorious coming will close "the latter days" and usher in the Millennial Age. If this be correct the *national* conversion of the Jews is not to be expected in "the latter days."

The "return" of the children of the Israel here depicted is not a return to Palestine, but to God and to David their king. Does this refer to a recovenanting under the Mosaic Covenant or under the New? The former alternative is very difficult to maintain.

What does "seeking David their king" mean? It seems capable of at least two interpretations.

First, the reference may be possibly to our Lord Jesus Christ, David's greater Son. This interpretation would preclude all idea of Israel being brought back at this time into the Mosaic Covenant.

Secondly, the reference may be to the dynasty and Royal House of David. When Israel becomes a Christian nation, she will at the same period come under the sway and rule of a monarch of David's line. To summarize Hosea's teaching on this subject: Israel is brought as a heathen and idolatrous people into "the Wilderness." There they are betrothed to God by a New Covenant, and become "the sons of the Living God," a Christian nation. They multiply into an innumerable host; expand into the world; and then enter into possession of the Land of Promise with their brethren of the house of Judah. There is no mistaking Hosea's teaching as to the religious condition of Israel at their restoration. Is not all this but the history of the Anglo-Saxon race?

II. ISAIAH'S PREDICTIONS

Isaiah's frequent prophetic references to Israel in "the islands" have already been noticed. Not only were "the islands" to be a place of safety and renewal, but they were also to be a place of great spiritual blessing. When in these "islands" Israel was to become a God-fearing and God-honouring people. Isaiah does not definitely speak of their either being under the Old or the New Covenant, but the descriptions represent a state of Christian blessedness.

"They shall lift up their voice, they shall sing for the majesty of the Lord, they shall cry aloud from the sea. Wherefore glorify ye the Lord in the fires, even the name of the Lord God of Israel in *the isles of the sea.* From *the uttermost part of the earth* have we heard songs, even glory to the righteous" (*Isaiah* 24:14-16).

The name of the God of Israel is to be glorified in "the isles" and from "the uttermost part of the earth" songs are to ascend to God.

"Sing unto the Lord a new song, and His praise from *the end of the earth* ..." (*Isaiah* 42:10).

Since this is to take place in the New Covenant times, it can hardly be a description of Israel taken back into favour under the Mosaic Covenant.

Isaiah 49 is a chapter of New Covenant blessing. It describes Israel in "the isles." In verse 3 we read that there God is to be glorified by Israel.

"Thou art My servant, O Israel, in whom I will be glorified" (*Isaiah* 49:3).

The fifty-fourth chapter of *Isaiah* is addressed to Israel of the Ten Tribes. Israel is described as the "barren" and "desolate" wife (verse 1), as the "woman forsaken" and the "refused wife of youth" (verse 6), whereas Judah is "the married wife." Judah at this time had not been carried captive—of her at this stage Hosea had said, "Judah yet ruleth with God and is faithful with the Saints" (*Hosea* 11:12). But Israel had been stricken and carried captive, and it is for her that the prophet foretells a glorious Restoration and much spiritual blessing:

"All thy children shall be taught of the Lord; and great shall be the peace of thy children" (*Isaiah* 54:13).

That this means Christian teaching is obvious from the reference made by our blessed Lord to this very passage (see *John* 6:44, 45).

III. JEREMIAH'S PREDICTIONS

The thirty-first chapter of *Jeremiah* deals almost entirely with the house of Israel, up to verse 31 solely with Israel. The prophet speaks of the captives finding grace in the Wilderness.

"At the same time, saith the Lord, will I be the God of all the families of Israel, and they shall be My people. Thus saith the Lord, The people which were left of the sword found *grace in the wilderness;* even Israel, when I went to cause him to rest" (*Jeremiah* 31:1, 2).

The period, "at the same time," has already been shown to be "the latter days" (*Jeremiah* 30:24). Hence the work of grace here spoken of is to be in the Christian dispensation, the dispensation of the New Covenant, that is before the Millennium. Israel, before the Second

Coming of the Messiah, is to find grace when recuperating in "the Wilderness." What does "finding grace" signify? Is it not the grace of the Gospel? Does it not mean a coming into the New Covenant? Does it not imply becoming a Christian nation? How closely do the blessings depicted here and in the following verses resemble the spiritual blessings predicted by Hosea. Israel was to be wooed in the wilderness as in Hosea's account:

"Yea, I have loved thee with an everlasting love: therefore with loving kindness have I drawn thee" (*Jeremiah* 31:3).

That this wilderness was to be the place of Israel's repentance and return to God is evidenced in verses 18 and 19, where the people of the northern kingdom are spoken of under the name of Ephraim.

The scriptures already examined have led to the conclusion that the Restoration of Israel in "the Wilderness" or "islands" could not be effected under the Old Covenant. In this same chapter, which speaks of "finding grace in the wilderness," the prophet Jeremiah goes on definitely to tell of the New Covenant:

"Behold, the days come, saith the Lord, that I will make a New Covenant with the house of Israel, and with the house of Judah ... But this shall be the Covenant that I will make with the house of Israel; After those days, saith the Lord, I will put my law in their inward parts, and write it in their hearts; and will be their God, and they shall be My people..." (*Jeremiah* 31:31, 33).

Note that Israel and Judah were to be two distinct peoples in the New Covenant times, and not merged, as too many think, into one single people, the Jews. The New Covenant is to be made with them both, but in verse 33 it is a striking fact that Judah is omitted and Israel alone is mentioned. Is not this significant? especially in view of the fact that Judah as a people had not yet come into the New Covenant, but rejecting it still continues under the Mosaic Law. Whereas Israel, as a Nation and a Company of Nations, is founded under this self-same New Covenant.

It is of interest to recall that in the service of the National Church of the Anglo-Saxon peoples, when the Commandments of God are recited, the people pray in the precise terms of the promised

Covenant, thus: "Lord, have mercy upon us, and write all these Thy laws in our hearts, we beseech Thee." They plead for a fulfilment of the gracious terms of the New Covenant made with Israel.

Jeremiah then teaches us that Israel was to become a Christian nation in "the Wilderness" before her Final Restoration with the Jews to the Promised Land. Israel was to be pre-eminently the New Covenant People, a much-ignored fact. The New Covenant was to be Israel's religion, appointed them by God, and made with none else, though all might have a glorious share in it. The Gentile believers are simply grafted into the Church of Israel through faith in Israel's Redeemer; they become partakers "of the root and fatness of the olive tree" (*Romans* 11:17).

IV. EZEKIEL'S PREDICTION

"As I live, saith the Lord God, surely with a mighty hand, and with a stretched out arm, and with fury poured out, will I rule over you; And I will bring you out from the people, and will gather you out of the countries wherein ye are scattered, with a mighty hand, and with a stretched out arm, and with fury poured out. And I will bring you into the wilderness of the people, and there will I plead with you face to face. Like as I pleaded with your fathers in the wilderness of the land of Egypt, so will I plead with you, saith the Lord God. And I will cause you to pass under the rod, and *I will bring you into the Bond of the Covenant*..." (*Ezekiel* 20:33-37).

Here is an account of the luring and bringing of Israel into "the Wilderness." In this place, and not in Palestine, does God "plead face to face" with Israel, wooing her and bringing her into a "Bond" of union with Himself. This depicts nothing but a national return to the true worship of Jehovah from all her idolatries. Not until Israel in "the Wilderness" has been brought again into Covenant relationship with God does she return to the Promised Land (see verse 42). According to Ezekiel, Israel must get right with God before the great and Final Restoration to the possession of Palestine.

What is this "Bond of the Covenant"? Surely that same which Hosea and Jeremiah described? It cannot be yet another? It must be the same in each case. There could be no return of Israel to the Old Covenant, for she had been once and for all "divorced" from under that bond. But not so Judah. Judah was never "divorced." This term is never used of the Jews, but of Israel only. If Israel is ever to be in Covenant with Jehovah again it must be under a New Bond, as a people not necessarily circumcised, and certainly not under the old Mosaic Covenant—a condition which, although so contrary to the generally accepted teaching on this subject, is true of the Anglo-Saxons.

V. ZECHARIAH'S PREDICTION

The prophet Zechariah prophesied some eighteen years after the return of the captivity from Babylon. In his tenth chapter we have these words concerning Israel:

"I will hiss for them, and gather them; for I have redeemed them; and they shall increase as they have increased. And I will sow them among the people: and they shall remember Me in far countries; and they shall live with their children, and turn again. I will bring them again also out of the land of Egypt, and gather them out of Assyria; and I will bring them into the land of Gilead and Lebanon; and place shall not be found for them" (*Zechariah* 10:8-10).

These words have nothing to do with the Jews, they refer wholly to Israel. This is evident from verse 7, where the Ten Tribes are spoken of under the term "Ephraim." We have in these verses:
1. A "gathering" together.
2. A "redeeming."
3. An increase in population
4. A "sowing."
5. A second gathering, or bringing into the Promised Land.

Note that in a place other than Palestine Israel is to "remember" God and "turn again" to Him. "They shall remember Me in far countries and they shall live with their children and turn again." This is the wooing in the "wilderness," the betrothal, the finding grace and the entry into the new marriage bond with God. The remembering and turning to God in *far countries* showed that the idolatrous nation, when far removed from Palestine, were to become a Christian people. There was therefore such a thing as spiritual blessing for Israel when far from Palestine, and it was after being thus abundantly blessed that they were to possess the land promised to their Fathers.

Is not the foregoing fulfilled in the history of the Anglo-Saxons in every particular? The Tribes gather and are brought into the Appointed Place, the Wilderness, the Islands, where they rest and consolidate. They then come into Covenant with God and become a Christian nation and are nationally redeemed. Shortly after this they multiply exceedingly and commence colonizing, they spread abroad, they are sown in the earth, and finally come into possession of the great Land promised to Abraham "from the river of Egypt to the great river Euphrates."

Zechariah certainly makes it clear that before possessing Palestine Israel must exist as a Christian nation in far-off regions.

According to these five prophets the religion of Israel before the Millennium, before the possession of Palestine, before reunion with the Jews, was that of the New Covenant. The New Covenant was the "Appointed Religion" of Israel in "the latter days."

Thus we have seen that the Anglo-Saxon race is found:

At Israel's "Appointed Time."

In Israel's "Appointed Place."

With Israel's "Appointed Religion."

If the conclusion be obvious, what should be our attitude?

"And the people believed: and when they heard that the Lord had visited the children of Israel, and that He had looked upon their affliction, then they bowed their heads and worshipped" (*Exodus* 4:31).

CHAPTER VI

THE POPULATION OF ISRAEL'S RESTORATION

CONTENTS

THE POPULATION OF ISRAEL'S RESTORATION

The Time, Place and Religion of Israel's Preliminary Restoration having been discussed, only a few additional details of her condition remain to be gathered from the various passages which have already been examined. Much, for instance, is said about the population of Israel at her Restoration. Immense population and expansion of the race are emphasized by the prophets, besides some very remarkable points regarding their colonial enterprise which have been fulfilled on a gigantic scale in the Anglo-Saxon race. Incidentally, this has been touched upon already at several points in the foregoing studies. Here we collect them together to view the subject as a whole.

As to population, what was to be the number of this people? At the time of their captivity and during the time of their punishment they were to be few in number and their population was to be relatively small. Their numbers when foregathering in the Appointed Place would be small and remain so until the Appointed Time for the ending of the Seven Times punishment. But what was it to be when the Restoration dawned, when the heavy, chastening hand of God was lifted from off His people? What were to be their numbers in the Isles?

HOSEA ON ISRAEL'S POPULATION

Hosea's teaching is beyond all possibility of doubt:

"Yet the number of the children of Israel shall be as *the sand of the sea, which cannot be measured nor numbered*" (*Hosea* 1:10).

This, it will be said, is the language of hyperbole. Granted; but what does the hyperbole signify? It stands for something definite, and does not mean the ordinary increase of population. It certainly means teeming population and phenomenal increase of the race.

In this connection may be recalled the words of the patriarch Jacob, when he blessed Ephraim and Manasseh, the sons of Joseph, the Birthright heir. In the latter days, the very period to which Hosea refers, their seed was to increase and swarm like fishes.

"The Angel which redeemed me from all evil, bless the lads; and let my name be named on them, and the name of my fathers Abraham and Isaac; and let them grow into a multitude in the midst of the earth" (*Genesis* 48:16).

In the marginal note, the words "let them grow into a multitude" are translated as "let them grow as fishes do increase." They were to send forth shoals of offspring, swarming and multiplying, just as fishes breed in the seas.

The words of Hosea, "as the sand of the sea," are exactly those used by God when the Promise was confirmed to Abraham by oath on Mount Moriah.

"By Myself have I sworn, saith the Lord, for because thou hast done this thing, and hast not withheld thy son, thine only son: That in blessing I will bless thee, and in multiplying I will multiply thy seed as the stars of heaven, and as *the sand which is upon the sea shore*" (*Genesis* 22:16).

This and other promises made to the Fathers were for fulfilment in "the Latter Days," the very same period in which the Restoration was to take place. Obviously, these great national blessings promised by God to the Fathers could not be enjoyed in that period of the Latter Days which was synchronous with the Seven Times Punishment, but only in the Latter Days after the termination of the great Punishment.

Hosea clearly shows that Israel was to be an exceedingly populous race when she entered into the possession of the Land of Promise and before her reunion with Judah.

In passing, note that this fact alone negatives any suggestion that Israel returned with the Jews on their return from captivity in Babylon.

Is it not arresting and suggestive that the people found at the Appointed Time in the Appointed Place with the Appointed Religion did multiply exceedingly as foretold by Hosea? Not one single item of these striking characteristics is wanting to the Anglo-Saxons. The phenomenal expansion of population began at the predestined hour.

An additional statement by Hosea concerning this prolific race is:

"And I will sow her unto Me in the earth" (*Hosea* 2:23).

As already seen, the latter half of Hosea's second chapter is devoted to Israel's Restoration. It was after being blest and increased in "the Wilderness" that God would "sow" her "in the earth." The figure indicates colonial expansion. Being "sown in the earth" is the spreading abroad and occupation of other lands. It is not the dispersion of a homeless people as was that of the Jews up till 1918, but an expansion in blessing and power. It was the spreading abroad promised to Jacob to the west, east, north, and south (*Genesis* 28:14). The expansion was to be in and from the Appointed Place. That Place did not include the great territories to which the race spread, it only comprises the British Isles.

ZECHARIAH ON ISRAEL'S POPULATION

The tenth chapter of Zechariah's prophecy has already come under review in the foregoing studies. On re-reading the passage, it will be found that reference is made to Israel's increase of population at the time of her Restoration, and also her colonial expansion:

"I will hiss for them, and gather them; for I have redeemed them: and *they shall increase* as they have increased. And *I will sow them* among the people" (*Zechariah* 10:8, 9).

This exactly corresponds with Hosea's reference to increase and consequent planting of colonies. In both passages the "sowing" is done by God Himself, and is a manifestation of His good favour upon the nationally pardoned and redeemed race. This colonial expansion was indicated centuries before when Jacob blessed the Birthright son, Joseph.

"Joseph is a fruitful bough, even a fruitful bough by a well; whose branches run over the wall" (*Genesis* 49:22).

This over-running of the branches was the encroachment upon the territories and lands of other peoples—a poetic description of colonial expansion. Zechariah simply repeats that this long-foretold colonization is to take place upon Israel's Restoration prior to her possession of Palestine.

"I will bring them again also out of the land of Egypt, and gather them out of Assyria; and I will bring them into the land of Gilead and Lebanon; and place shall not be found for them" (*Zechariah* 10:10).

When, with Judah, the Ten Tribes once again possess the Land of Promise, they will be such a countless host in all the earth that the Promised Land will not be able to hold and sustain them all, thus clearly showing that they will not all move in Palestine, but only occupy it representatively. Furthermore, we learn from yet another prophet, Jeremiah, that the return will only be representative.

"Turn, O backsliding children, saith the Lord; for I am married unto you: and I will take you one of a city, and two of a family, and I will bring you to Zion" (*Jeremiah* 3:14).

Further, when God made promise of the Appointed Place for Israel, did He not make it clear and plain that it was no temporary home, but a perpetual abode in addition to Palestine, one that they would not give up, even when they once more possessed the Land promised to their Fathers?

"Moreover I will appoint a place for My people Israel and will plant them, that they may dwell in a place of their own, and *move no more*; neither shall the children of wickedness afflict them any more as before time" (II *Samuel* 7:10).

God gave to Israel a place and home other than and in addition to the Land of Promise, whereas to the Jews He has given but one national home. This is one of the great differences between Israel and Judah.

ISAIAH ON THE POPULATION OF ISRAEL

The fifty-fourth chapter of *Isaiah* has already been cited as one descriptive of Israel's Restoration. The prolific expansion of numbers is thus touched upon;

"Sing, O barren, thou that didst not bear; break forth into singing, and cry aloud, thou that didst not travail with child: for more are the children of the desolate than the children of the married wife, saith the Lord" (*Isaiah* 54:1).

The prophecy states that the progeny of Israel, described as the "barren" and "desolate" wife, was to be far more numerous than the children of Judah, the "married wife." The verse refers to the time when the desolation of Israel should cease, when the Seven Times Punishment should end. In that day, remarried to God, the nation is to begin its career of expansion, and multiplicity of seed is to characterize the people. The next verse emphasizes this multitudinousness:

"Enlarge the place of thy tent, and let them stretch forth the curtains of thine habitations: spare not, lengthen thy cords, and strengthen thy stakes" (*Isaiah* 54:2).

Breaking Forth

The land of their Restoration, the Appointed Place, becomes overcrowded, it is necessary to enlarge the home. Verse 3 continues this picture of increase in numbers, and opens up a vision of colonization.

"For thou shalt break forth on the right hand and on the left; and thy seed shall inherit the Gentiles, and make the desolate cities to be inhabited" (*Isaiah* 54:3).

The "breaking forth" is the "spreading abroad" to the west, east, north, and south. It is the being sown in the earth. The seed is to "inherit the Gentiles." Here is the role and destiny of Israel. The time for the performance of this programme is fully come, yea overdue. The Jews are not filling this role because it is not theirs to fill. Where is the Restored Israel? What race is fulfilling her destiny? What people is inheriting the Gentiles? and has been filling this predestined role from the very date of the cessation of Israel's Seven Times Punishment? The seed is to "make the desolate cities to be inhabited." How great a part Israel was destined to play on the world's stage!

How comes it about that another race (if indeed it be another) is fulfilling the predicted destiny of Israel?

The remaining part of the chapter is full of import to our race. We subjoin five verses:

"Fear not; for thou shalt not be ashamed: neither be thou confounded; for thou shalt not be put to shame: for thou shalt forget the shame of thy youth, and shalt not remember the reproach of thy widowhood any more. For thy Maker is thine husband; The Lord of hosts is His name; and thy Redeemer the Holy One of Israel; The God of the whole earth shall He be called.

For the Lord hath called thee as a woman forsaken and grieved in spirit, and a wife of youth, when thou wast refused, saith thy God.

For a small moment have I forsaken thee; but *with great mercies will I gather thee.*

In a little wrath I hid My face from thee for a moment; but *with everlasting kindness will I have mercy on thee,* saith the Lord thy Redeemer" (*Isaiah* 54:4-8).

These verses tell of the gathering of Israel, of the nation's redemption, and betrothal to God. They tell, in short, of a very blessed Restoration, though it be not the yet greater one to follow.

Loss of the First Child

Reference was previously made to the forty-ninth chapter of *Isaiah* as being one that told of Israel's Preliminary Restoration. It is a chapter that concerns the Ten Tribes, and these remarkable statements are made concerning them.

"The children which thou shalt have, after thou hast lost the other, shall say again in thine ears, The place is too strait for me: give place to me that I may dwell. Then shalt thou say in thine heart, Who hath begotten me these, seeing I have lost my children, and am desolate, a captive, and removing to and fro? and who hath brought up these? Behold, I was left alone; these, where had they been?" (*Isaiah* 49:20, 21.)

This is a vivid picture of surprising increase of population, and of consequent great colonial development on the part of Israel. It repeats what was taught by other prophets as to increase in numbers. But in addition there is disclosed here a detailed and curious history. The ordinary chances of such a thing happening at the end of 2,520 years are infinitesimal. The first child or first colony is to be lost to Israel. Then she is to have more children, and these, owing to the overcrowding in the old home, the motherland, cry out for fresh lands and homes for growth and extension. It reads as if Israel was not to lose any of her later children after the first.

Where is this Israel? The hour for her entrance on to the world's stage struck nigh a century ago. She ought to be playing her great role. God is never behind time in the performance of His word. Is the British Anglo-Saxon race only an understudy? Or merely a stop-gap or *locum tenens*?

The question needs to be asked because this prophetic utterance concerning Israel is a literal statement of British colonial history. When Israel's Appointed Time drew nigh, this British nation began to multiply exceedingly. The first colonial enterprise was, as foretold, to the west, to America. The first colony was lost to it by the secession of the United States. Since losing that colony it has had several others, such as Canada, Australia, New Zealand, and South Africa, which have now grown into great self-governing Dominions, all uniting with the mother-country to form the British Empire, the Fifth great World-Empire of Nebuchadnezzar's dream, an empire that was to stand for ever.

If the British Empire, with the United States, be not Israel, if it is only a portion of the Fourth (Roman) Empire, if it is only one of the Ten Toe Kingdoms, as some firmly believe, how comes it that it is playing the exact part of Israel? How is it that it has become the New Covenant people?

The secession of the United States of America from Britain has had the effect of dividing the one kindred race into two distinct sections, consisting on the one hand of the motherland, the British Isles and her five great daughter Dominions beyond the Seas, forming a Nation and a Company of Nations, all under a monarchy and making a mighty empire, while on the other hand is the Republic of the United States of America, forming a great people, and curiously enough, not under a monarchy. How utterly wrong things would have been had they had a king!

The astounding thing is that this very grouping was foretold concerning Israel in the scriptures some centuries before Isaiah lived and prophesied. When Jacob blessed the two sons of the heir to the stupendous Birthright, he looked down the long vista of the centuries into "the Latter Days" and saw for the lads a glowing future. That of Ephraim was to be "*a multitude of nations*," and Manasseh, "*a people, great.*"

"And he blessed Joseph and said, God, before whom my fathers Abraham and Isaac did walk, the God which fed me all my life long unto this day, the Angel which redeemed me from all evil, bless the lads; and let my name be named on them, and the name of my fathers Abraham and Isaac; and *let them grow into a multitude in the midst of the earth.*

And when Joseph saw that his father laid his right hand upon the head of Ephraim, it displeased him: and he held up his father's hand, to remove it from Ephraim's head unto Manasseh's head. And Joseph said unto his father, Not so, my father: for this is the firstborn: put thy right hand upon his head. And his father refused, and said, I know it: he also shall become *a people,* and he also shall be *great*: but truly his younger brother shall be greater than he, and his seed shall *become a multitude of nations*..." (*Genesis* 48:15-19).

Manasseh was to be one single great people, and Ephraim was to consist of several distinct nations, a Commonwealth of Nations. How unlikely of fulfilment was this curious prophecy! It was for fulfilment in the Latter Days, and, behold, in the fulness of time we have the very state of affairs before our eyes!

The loss of the first colony, this secession of the United States from Britain, must not be regarded as an unfortunate schism or as a fatal blunder. Not at all. It was but the preordained course for Israel. It may have been brought about by the unwisdom and folly of man, but the folly was overruled by God, and this great rending was His doing just as much as was the rending of the kingdom on the death of Solomon. "It was a thing that was brought about of the Lord" (I *Kings* 12:15, R.V.) and "This thing is from Me" (I *Kings* 12:24). Both events were to work out the great Divine purpose of blessing for humanity.

These two sections of the Anglo-Saxon race must sooner or later combine to carry out the great vocation of Israel. No material bonds can possibly produce such an effective brotherly union as a full realization that God has predestined them to be His Servant, to serve the nations, to guide, help, protect, and succour them with all their resources and sympathy, and to lead them into the paths of justice and judgment.

The destiny of the race is indeed great; high and holy is the calling. It is no light matter for a people to be the elected Servant of Jehovah, as was Israel. Such an election is no ground for pride or vainglory. Rightly understood, it can be no incentive to foolish boasting, but rather should it cause holy awe at the magnitude of the service to be rendered and at the unfitness of the Servant called upon to render it.

Well may we be humbled by the contemplation of our national and individual sins. Straitened indeed are we in ourselves, "to us belongeth confusion of face…because we have sinned against Thee." But we are not straitened in our God, in His hand the race will not fail of His purpose. It was ever known that Israel could only effectively witness and serve through the outpouring of God's Spirit upon the people. For this enduement we wait; it has been promised, it must come.

Further, since God has foretold that Israel and Judah are to be united once again, a mighty and irresistible union of the Jews, the British Empire, and the United States of America is involved in the near future—a combination of all that is best on earth for the temporal and spiritual benefit of humanity.

Little wonder that Moses, looking down the long ages and foreseeing the ultimate destiny of the chosen people in the latter days, exclaimed, "Oh that they were wise, that they understood this, that they would consider their latter end."

As the Lord spoke through Isaiah . . .

"Thou, Israel, My Servant, Jacob whom I have chosen, the seed of Abraham My friend; thou whom I

have taken hold of from the ends of the earth, and called thee from the corners thereof, and said unto thee:-

Thou art My Servant, I have chosen thee and not cast thee away; fear thou not, for I am with thee; be not dismayed, for I am Thy God: I will strengthen thee; yea, I will help thee; yea, I will uphold thee with the right hand of My righteousness"

(Isaiah 41:8-10, R.V.)

INDEX

G

Germany, 29
Golden Calves, 8
Gospel Dispensation, 19
Gozan, River of, 11

H

Halah and Habor, 11
History of the Various Isles, 50
Hosea, Prophet to Israel, 10
    Foretold Punishment, 10
    Foretold Restoration, 20
    on wilderness, 39
Hosea's Three Days, 10, 23, 24, 25, 28, 30, 31
    Third Day, 10, 19, 22-26, 56
    Second Day, 56

I

Isaiah, 11
    on Wilderness, 42
    on Islands, 43, 47-55
Islands, Isles, 35; ch. IV. 47-55
    by Isaiah, 43
    by Jeremiah, 48
    Coastlands, 49
    Beyond the Sea, 54
    not in Mediterranean, 54
Isles of the Sea, 51, 52, 53
    of the West, 52
Israel, Double meaning, 7
Israel and Judah, Distinction, 36, 48, 65, 74
Israel in Europe, 11
Israel Devoured, Swallowed up, 27
Israel's Religious Decline, 8, 59

J

Jeremiah on Wilderness, 39, 40
    on Islands, 48, 49
Jeroboam, 8
Jewish Kingdom, 7, 12
Jezreel, 10
Jonah, 27
    Third Day, 27
Jutes, 55

L

Latter, Last Days, 19, 20, 21, 24, 25, 27, 31, 62, 64, 72, 78
    by Hosea, 20
    by Jeremiah, 20, 21
    Limits of, 19
    Termination of, 19
Lengthening the Cords, 75
Lo-Ammi, 10
Lo-Ruhamah, 10
Loss of First Child, 76, 77

M

Manasseh, 71, 78
Married Wife, 64
Mediterranean Sea, 49, 51, 54
Migration into Europe, 11
Millennium, 19
Mosaic Covenant (The Old), 8, 59, 63
Multitude of Nations, 78

N

Napoleon, 29
Nation and Company of Nations, 78

FURTHER READING

A Synopsis of the Migrations of Israel
by W.E. Filmer

God's Great Plan
by R. Llewelyn Williams

God's Great Week
by J.S. Fox

The Master Plan
by A.S. Gaunt

The Lost Tribes of Israel FAQs
by J. Martin Lightfoot

All books from Covenant Publishing